MORE
ONE MINUTE
NONSENSE

ANTHONY DE MELLO, S.J.

MORE

ONE MINUTE
NONSENSE

A Campion Book

LOYOLA UNIVERSITY PRESS
CHICAGO

©1993 Loyola University Press
U.S. and Canadian edition
All rights reserved
Printed in the United States of America

©1992 Gujarat Sahitya Prakash, Anand, India
Original English edition

Loyola University Press
3441 North Ashland Avenue
Chicago, Illinois 60657

Library of Congress Cataloging-in-Publication Data
De Mello, Anthony, 1931-
 More one minute nonsense / Anthony de Mello.
  p.   cm. — (A Campion book)
 ISBN 0-8294-0749-9
 1. Meditations.   I. Title.
 BX2182.2.D3874   1993
 242—dc20   92-35241
                                           CIP

Cover and interior design by Nancy Gruenke.
The cover was adapted from the cover for *Contact with God:
Retreat Conferences* (Anthony de Mello, S.J. [Chicago: Loyola
University Press, 1991]) by Beth Herman Design Associates.

A NOTE FROM
THE AMERICAN PUBLISHER

Tony de Mello's last posthumous publication,
One Minute Nonsense, was originally published
in India as a one-volume edition. Loyola
University Press has chosen to make it available
as two books, including the present volume,
More One Minute Nonsense, and the previous
volume, *One Minute Nonsense.* This is partly
to stretch out, if we could, our leave-taking
of a contemporary author whose spirit, stories,
and imagery profoundly enriched the terms
of spiritual reflection today.

Father X. Diaz del Rio, S.J., director of Gujarat
Sahitya Prakash, the original publisher of *One
Minute Nonsense* (1992), did a favor to all the
readers and lovers of Father de Mello's work
when he wrote the following preface, taking us
through some of the last days of this remarkable
mentor:

> We are bringing out the last
> posthumous book of Tony de Mello,
> *One Minute Nonsense.*
>
> Actually he wrote it after *One Minute
> Wisdom* and before *The Prayer of the*

Frog. He sent the manuscript to the
publisher with instructions to print
it soon. It was as it appears now: the
stories had no titles and there was no
table of contents. The text was typed,
except the short commentary to the first
story that was handwritten by him.
The typesetting was about to start when
at the end of 1986 he wrote again:
"I am writing another book, which will
be entitled *The Prayer of the Frog,* and
it has to appear before *One Minute
Nonsense;* please send the manuscript
back to me."

In the early months of 1987 Tony
worked hard on *The Prayer of the Frog.*
He wanted to hand over the manuscript
for publication before his departure for
New York at the end of May. I met Tony
in Bombay on May 30. We discussed
the layout of the book for several hours.
After completing that work I asked
Tony about the manuscript of *One
Minute Nonsense.* He told me that it
was ready and he would send it to
me immediately on his return from
America. After that he would start
preparing a book of meditations.

At about six o'clock that evening
I wished Tony goodbye and left to catch
my train back to Gujarat. Two hours
later he himself left for the airport.
He died at Fordham University, the
very night of his first day in New York,
June 1, 1987.

He never expected to be back so
soon. His body arrived in the morning
of June 13 and was buried the same
evening in the cemetery at St. Peter's
Church, Bandra, where he had been
baptized.

Among his papers . . . *One Minute
Nonsense* [was found]. "Ready for the
press" he had said, but the stories had
no title and there was no table of
contents. Did he intend to add them?
We shall never know; but probably not,
since he told me "it is ready for the
press."

And so we are bringing out his last
book, *One Minute Nonsense,* the one he
wanted to come after *The Prayer of the
Frog.* We publish it as he left it, without
titles and without contents, just the

stories, one after the other, in the same
order in which he left them.

Our thanks to Father del Rio, not only as the
original publisher of a number of Father de
Mello's books but for the personal report above.
Father de Mello was not only the complete
professional. He inspired friendship broadly
and tears from many when the Lord took him
home on short notice.

Rev. Joseph F. Downey, S.J.
Editorial Director
Loyola University Press

"The man talks nonsense," said a visitor after hearing the Master speak.

Said a disciple, "You would talk nonsense too if you were trying to express the Inexpressible."

> When the visitor checked this out with the Master himself, this is the reply he got: "No one is exempt from talking nonsense. The great misfortune is to do it solemnly."

From the manuscript handwritten by Fr. de Mello

The Master in these tales is not a single person. He is a Hindu guru, a Zen roshi, a Taoist sage, a Jewish rabbi, a Christian monk, a Sufi mystic. He is Lao Tzu and Socrates, Buddha and Jesus, Zarathustra and Mohammed. His teaching is found in the seventh century B.C. and the twentieth century A.D. His wisdom belongs to East and West alike. Do his historical antecedents really matter? History, after all, is the record of appearances, not Reality; of doctrines, not of Silence.

It will only take a minute to read each of the anecdotes that follow. You will probably find the Master's language baffling, exasperating, even downright meaningless. This, alas, is not an easy book! It was written, not to instruct, but to Awaken. Concealed within its pages (not in the printed words, not even in the tales, but in its spirit, its mood, its atmosphere) is a Wisdom that cannot be conveyed in human speech. As you read the printed page and struggle within the Master's cryptic language it is possible that you will unwittingly chance upon the Silent Teaching that lurks within the book, and be Awakened—and transformed. This is what Wisdom means: To be changed without the slightest effort on your part, to be transformed, believe it or not, merely by waking to the reality that is not words, that lies beyond the reach of words.

If you are fortunate enough to be Awakened thus, you will know why the finest language is the one that is not spoken, the finest action is the one that is not done, and the finest change is the one that is not willed.

Caution: Take the tales in tiny doses—one or two at a time. An overdose will lower their potency.

MORE ONE MINUTE NONSENSE

The Master made sure the monastery library
was well stocked with books on every
conceivable subject—politics, architecture,
philosophy, poetry, agriculture, history, science,
psychology, art . . . and the section he himself
used the most, fiction.

His one refrain was, "God save us from people
who do not THINK, THINK, THINK!"

There was nothing he feared more, he said, than
the one-track mind, the one-book fanatic.

This puzzled the disciples for it was so out
of tune with the non-thinking perception,
the non-conceptual awareness, that was the
mainstay of the Master's teaching.

When asked directly, this was his ambiguous
reply: "A thorn can be dislodged by means
of another thorn, can't it?"

The Master had a large skull-and-bones
CAUTION sign set up in the monastery library.
It read: BOOKS KILL.

"Why?" someone wanted to know.

"Because books breed ideas that can freeze into
beliefs thereby causing a hardening of the mind
and a distorted perception of Reality."

A disciple complained about the Master's habit of knocking down all his cherished beliefs.

Said the Master:

"I set fire to the temple of your beliefs, for when it is destroyed you will have an unimpeded view of the vast, unbounded sky."

The Master met a very old neighbor shuffling along with a cane in his hand.

"Good morning," he called out. "And how are you these days?"

"Not well," said the man in a feeble voice. "I used to walk around the block every morning before breakfast. Now I feel so weak I can only get halfway and then have to turn around and come back."

The Master stressed awareness over worship.

"But must we not depend on God?" he was asked.

Said the Master, "The Lover desires the good of the beloved—which requires, among other things, the liberation of the beloved from the Lover."

Later he enacted an imaginary dialogue between God and his devotee:

Devotee: Please don't leave me, God.

God: I go so that the holy spirit may come.

Devotee: What's this holy spirit?

God: The fearlessness and freedom that comes from nondependence.

The Master once told of a neighbor in the countryside who had an obsession with acquiring land.

"I wish I had more land," he said one day.

"But why?" asked the Master. "Don't you have enough already?"

"If I had more land I could raise more cows."

"And what would you do with them?"

"Sell them and make money."

"For what?"

"To buy more land and raise a lot of cows . . ."

The preacher took issue with the Master on the
matter of dependence on God.

"God is our father," he said, "and we never cease
to need his help."

Said the Master, "When a father helps his infant
child, all the world smiles. When a father helps
his grown-up child, all the world weeps!"

The Master had very definite views on family
planning. For all those who contended that the
size of a family was the private concern of
parents or the internal affair of a country, he
had the following parable:

> There was once a country where
> it became possible for everyone to
> develop and acquire their own nuclear
> bombs—small ones, the size of hand
> grenades, but powerful enough to blow
> up an entire city.

> A bitter debate raged over the right
> of private citizens to possess such
> explosives—till they came to the
> following compromise: No one would
> be allowed to carry a nuclear bomb in
> public without a license. But what
> people did in their homes was their own
> private concern.

Someone told the Master of the phenomenal increase in the circulation of a sex magazine.

"Too bad," was his comment. "Of Sex as Reality it may be said that the more you read about it the less you know it."

Later he added, "And the less you enjoy it."

"The modern world is suffering increasingly from sexual anorexia," said the psychiatrist.

"What's that?" said the Master.

"A loss of appetite for sex."

"How terrible!" said the Master. "What's the cure for it?"

"We don't know. Do you?"

"I think I do."

"What?"

"Make sex a sin again," said the Master with an impish smile.

While the Master did not oppose the practice of psychotherapy and even claimed that it was necessary for some people, he made no secret of his opinion that a psychotherapist merely brings relief; he does not really solve your problem—he merely exchanges it for another, more comfortable, one.

He recalled sitting in a bus after the war, intrigued to see a passenger holding a heavy object wrapped in a newspaper.

"What's that you've got on your lap?" the bus conductor demanded.

"An unexploded bomb. I'm taking it to the fire department."

"Heavens above, man! You don't want to carry a thing like that on your lap! Put it under your seat!"

On voting day the Master would always be the first to show up at the polling booth.

He could never understand why some of the disciples failed to exercise their right to vote.

"People are ready to pay their taxes and shed their blood for democracy," he said. "Why will they not take the trouble to vote and make it work?"

The Master had this story to tell about the way people look at other people.

Soon after his marriage he lived for a while on the tenth floor of a city apartment. His young wife one day stepped out of the shower to reach for the towel when she froze. There outside the window was a window washer looking at her. A whole minute passed as she stood there rooted to the ground, too stunned to move a muscle.

The man broke the spell. "What's the matter, lady?" he said. "Haven't you seen a window washer before?"

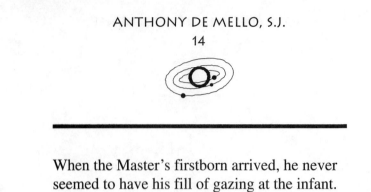

When the Master's firstborn arrived, he never seemed to have his fill of gazing at the infant.

"What do you want him to be when he grows up?" someone asked.

"Outrageously happy," said the Master.

"Congratulate me!"

"Why?"

"At last I've found a job that offers excellent prospects for advancement."

Said the Master somberly, "You were a sleepwalker yesterday. You are sleepwalking today. You will sleepwalk till the day you die. What sort of advancement is that?"

"It was financial advancement I was talking about, not spiritual advancement."

"Ah! I see. A sleepwalker with a bank account that he isn't awake to enjoy!"

"Enlightenment," said the Master when asked
about it, "is an awakening."

"Right now you are asleep and do not know it."

Then he went on to tell them of the recently
married woman who complained about her
husband's drinking habits.

"If you knew he drank, why did you marry
him?" she was asked.

"I had no idea he drank," said the woman, "till
one night he came home sober!"

Jesus set up the birds of the air and the flowers
of the field as models for humans to imitate.
So did the Master. He often told of the letter he
received from an affluent neighbor that read:

"Dear Sir,

This concerns the birdbath that I donated to the
monastery garden. I'm writing to inform you
that it is not to be used by the sparrows."

A visitor, in the course of explaining his religion to the Master, said, "We believe we are God's chosen people."

"What does that mean?" said the Master.

"That God chose us from among all the peoples of the earth."

"I think I can guess who, from among all the people of the earth, made that discovery," said the Master drily.

"Allow me to explain the Good News my
religion proclaims," said the preacher.

The Master was all attention.

"God is love. And He loves and rewards us
forever if we observe His commandments."

"IF?" said the Master. "Then the news isn't all
that good, is it?"

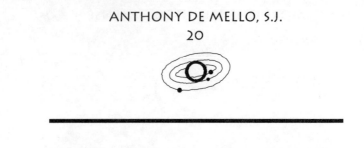

A badly wrapped parcel of Bibles arrived at the post office and burst open, scattering beautiful calf-bound, gilt-edged books all over the floor.

A postman could not resist the temptation to help himself to one.

When he confessed this later, the Master said, "But what on earth made you steal a Bible?"

"My religious disposition," said the man contritely.

"Some people claim there is no life after death," said a disciple.

"Do they?" said the Master noncommittally.

"Wouldn't it be awful to die—and never again see or hear or love or move?"

"You find that awful?" said the Master. "But that's how most people are even before they die."

A disciple decided to be more personal and direct.

"Do you believe in life after death?" she asked.

"Strange that you should be so stuck to that topic!" said the Master.

"Why would you think it strange?"

"Here you have this glorious April day in front of you," said the Master, pointing to the window, "like a child who refuses to eat today because he does not know what tomorrow will bring. You're starving. Eat your daily bread!"

The Master would sometimes regale visitors
with tales of the redoubtable Mullah Nasruddin.

Nasruddin was once tossing about in bed. Said
his wife, "What's the matter? Go to sleep!"

The mullah confessed he did not have the seven
silver coins he owed his neighbor Abdullah and
had to pay the following day. So he was too
worried to be able to sleep.

His wife promptly got up, threw a shawl round
her shoulders, went across the street, and
shouted, "Abdullah! Abdullah!" till old
Abdullah came to the window rubbing his eyes
sleepily and asking, "What is it? What's the
matter?"

The woman called out, "I just want you to know
you are not going to get your silver coins
tomorrow. My husband doesn't have them."

With that she walked back home and said, "Go
to sleep, Nasruddin. Now Abdullah can worry."

The Master concluded, "Someone has to pay.
Does anyone have to worry?"

To protect their crops the farmers had killed
countless numbers of birds. As he watched their
dead bodies strewn all over the place a disciple
recalled the saying of Jesus: "Not one of these
birds falls to the ground without your Father's
consent," and asked the Master if that sentence
made any sense.

"Yes, it does," said the Master. "But those words
reveal their inner beauty only if seen against
the background of these birds that breed by the
million and are then slaughtered as pests."

"What, concretely, is Enlightenment?"

"Seeing reality as it is."

"Doesn't everyone see Reality as it is?"

"Oh, no! Most people see it as they think it is."

"What's the difference?"

"The difference between thinking you are
drowning in a stormy sea—and knowing you
cannot drown because there isn't any water
in sight for miles around."

A psychiatrist came to see the Master.

"How do you deal with neurotics?" he asked.

Said the Master, "I liberate them."

"But how?"

"Rather than solve their problem I dissolve the ego that caused it."

"How could I myself do that?"

"Get out of the prison of your thoughts into the world of the senses," said the Master.

When the preacher returned to the Good News theme the Master interrupted him:

"What sort of Good News is it," he asked, "that makes it so easy to go to hell and so hard to get to heaven?"

To illustrate the fact that there simply aren't
any satisfactory symbols for God, the Master
told of the time his wife was driving him
through a crowded city street.

She collided with an approaching car whose
driver rolled his window down and yelled,
"Lady, why didn't you signal what you wanted
to do?"

"Because," she answered defiantly, "there is no
signal for what I wanted to do."

One day the Master looked at the preacher
sitting there in front of him, smug in his beliefs,
self-righteous in his good deeds, and he said,
"My friend, I sometimes feel that when you
come to die, you will die without ever having
lived—it will be as if life has passed you by."

Then, as an afterthought, he added, "No—it's
worse than that: Life and you have gone in
opposite directions."

The Master was certainly no stranger to what goes on in the world.

When asked to explain one of his favorite sayings,

> There is no good or ill but thinking makes it so,

this is what he said:

"Have you ever observed that what people call congestion in a train becomes atmosphere in a nightclub?"

To illustrate the same axiom he one day told how, as a child, he overheard his father, a famous politician, sharply criticize a party member who had crossed over to the opposition.

"But, Father, the other day you were all praise for the man who left the opposition to join your party."

"Well, Son, you might as well learn this important truth early in life: Those who go over to the other party are traitors. Those who come to ours are converts."

"In the land of Enlightenment your learning is
of as little use as clubs are in modern warfare.
What is needed here is awareness," said the
Master.

And he followed that statement up with the
story of a disciple who hired a Latvian refugee
as a housemaid, then found to her dismay that
the girl couldn't run a vacuum cleaner, operate
a mixer, or cope with a washing machine.

"What can you do?" she asked in desperation.

The girl smiled in quiet pride. "I can milk
a reindeer," she said.

"How long will it take me to solve my problem?"

"Not one minute more than it takes you to understand it," said the Master.

The preacher was an unusual man. People
trembled when they saw him. He never laughed
and was tenacious in his ascetical practices for
he believed in self-inflicted pain. He was
known to fast frequently and to wear scanty
clothing in the winter.

One day he confided to the Master a secret
pain: "I have lived a life of abnegation and been
faithful to precepts of my religion. But there's
something that eludes me, and I cannot find out
what. Can you?"

The Master looked at him, so hard and dry, and
said, "Yes. Soul."

Here is a tale the Master told a philosopher who demanded to know why cleverness was an obstacle to Enlightenment.

There were only three passengers in the plane—Big Brain, a boy scout, and a bishop. The plane developed engine trouble, and the pilot announced he was bailing out; there were only three parachutes, and he was taking one. The others would have to decide which of them was going to be saved. Big Brain said, "Since I am necessary to the country I take it for granted that I should have a parachute." So he grabbed one and jumped out.

The bishop looked at the boy scout and said, "Son, I have lived a long life, so I think it fitting that you should have the remaining parachute. I am ready to die."

"That won't be necessary, bishop," said the boy scout. "There are two parachutes here. Big Brain just jumped out with my knapsack."

Added the Master, "Cleverness ordinarily leaves no room for awareness."

Visitors were always struck by the Master's leisurely manner.

"I just don't have the time to be in a hurry," he would say.

"Aren't you going to wish us a Merry Christmas?"

The Master glanced at the calendar, saw it was a Thursday, and said, "I'd much rather wish you a happy Thursday."

This offended the Christians in the monastery till the Master explained, "Millions will enjoy, not Today, but Christmas—so their joy is short-lived. But for those who have learned to enjoy Today, every day is Christmas."

To a group of social activists who sought his blessing on a plan they were about to put into action, the Master said: "What you need, I'm afraid, is light, not action."

Later he explained, "To fight evil with activity is like fighting darkness with one's hands. So what you need is light, not fight."

It was quite impossible to get the Master to take
the idea of patriotism or nationalism seriously.

He once told of an Englishman who was
upbraided by a relative for becoming an
American citizen: "What have you gained
by becoming an American?"

"Well," said the other, "for one thing, I win
the American Revolution."

The Master once gave an address on the danger of religion, affirming, among other things, that religious people all too easily use God to cover up their pettiness and self-seeking.

This provoked a sharp rejoinder—in the form of a book wherein as many as a hundred religious leaders wrote articles to refute the Master's words.

The Master smiled when he saw the book. "If what I said was wrong, one article would have been enough," he said.

After delivering a stirring political speech at
a rally a disciple asked the Master what he
thought of it. Said the Master, "If what you said
was true where was the need to shout?"

And later, to all the disciples:

"Truth suffers more from the heat of its
defenders than from all the attacks of its
opponents."

The Master once exposed his disciples by means of the following advice:

He gave each of them a sheet of paper and asked them to write down the length of the hall they were in.

Almost everyone gave flat figures like fifty feet. Two or three added the word *approximately*.

Said the Master, "No one has given the right answer."

"What is the right answer?" they asked.

"The right answer is I DO NOT KNOW," said the Master.

The Master deplored the evils of competition.

"Doesn't competition bring out the best in us?"
he was asked.

"It brings out the worst because it teaches you
to hate."

"Hate what?"

"Yourself—for you allow your activity to be
determined by your competitor, not by your
own needs and limitations. Others—for you
seek to get ahead at their expense."

"But that would sound the death-knell of change
and progress," someone protested.

Said the Master, "The only progress there is,
is love-progress. The only change worth having
is a change of heart."

"Why do more people not attain
Enlightenment?" someone asked the Master.

"Because they see as loss what is actually
a gain."

Then he told of an acquaintance who went
into business. Trade flourished. There was
a constant run of customers.

When the Master congratulated him on how
well he was doing, the man said mournfully,
"Let's take a realistic view of things, sir. Look
at those front doors. If so many people continue
to push through them we'll soon have to replace
the hinges."

To a merchant who escaped from the pain of life into moneymaking, the Master said, "There was once a man who feared his own footprints. So, instead of walking, he took to running— which only increased the number of footprints he made. What he needed to do was stop."

"My suffering is unbearable."

Said the Master, "The present moment is never unbearable. It is what you think is coming in the next five minutes or the next five days that drives you to despair. Stop living in the future."

When asked what kind of a funeral he wanted for himself, the Master said, "Leave my body in a desert place and do not bother to dig a grave, so earth and sky will be my coffin, the moon and stars my funeral lamps, and all creation the funeral flowers."

"We'd rather cremate your body," said the disciples.

"That would be too much trouble," said the Master. "And why deprive the kites and ants of a funeral banquet?"

When someone announced he had become
a doctor of theology the Master, who was quite
a tease, said with an innocent air, "A doctor of
theology? What kind of disease is that?"

It was well known that the Master had little use for *theology,* as the word is commonly understood.

When asked point blank about it he said, "Theology has become an evil because it is not so much a quest for Truth as the maintenance of a belief system."

The Master held that the loyalty of theologians
to their belief systems made them all too prone
to turn a blind eye to the Truth—and reject the
Messiah when he appeared.

Philosophers fared better at his hands. Being
unfettered by beliefs, they were more open
in their quest, he said.

But even philosophy, alas, was limited for
it relied on words and concepts to penetrate
a Reality that was susceptible only to the
non-conceptualizing mind.

"Philosophy," he once remarked, "is a disease
that is cured only by Enlightenment. Then
it gives way to parables and silence."

"Why is it so hard for a rich man to enter the Kingdom of God?"

In reply the Master told of a man who arrived at a hotel in his limousine and was being carried to his room on a stretcher. The manager, thinking the man was paralysed, asked his wife what the matter was. The woman replied, "He's a very rich man. He doesn't need to walk."

The disciples told the Master of the epitaph they had designed for him:

IT WAS EASIER
TO BE FEARLESS
WHEN HE WAS AROUND.

Said the Master, "If in order to be fearless you needed me, my presence only served to conceal your cowardice, not to cure it."

The governor announced that he was coming to see a monastery bush that was full of exotic roses.

When he got to the monastery garden he found there was only one rose on the bush. When he learned that it was the Master who had cut all the other roses he demanded to know why.

"Because," said the Master, "had I left them on the bush you would not have seen even one of them."

Then, after a pause, he added, "You have grown accustomed to multitudes, my friend. When did you last see a person?"

"What must I do to attain the divine?"

"The divine isn't something one attains through doing, but something one realizes through seeing."

"What then is the function of doing?"

"To express the divine, not to attain it."

This is how the Master illustrated the attitude
of affluent nations today:

> A man is awakened from sleep by the
> nudgings of his wife: "Get up and close
> the window. It is freezing outside."

> The man sighs: "For heaven's sake!
> If I close the window will that make
> it warm outside?"

The Master would allow his disciples to live
with him only for a limited period of time; then
he would push them away to fend for
themselves.

When a newcomer questioned a disciple about
this practice of the Master, this is the reply he
got: "The Master is a mirror that reflects Reality
and you. Once you have seen Reality the mirror
must be flung away lest, through your
veneration, it turn into a screen."

"How can I change myself?"

"You are yourself—so you can no more change *yourself* than you can walk away from your feet."

"Is there nothing I can do then?"

"You can understand and accept this."

"How will I change if I accept myself?"

"How will you change if you don't? What you don't accept you do not *change,* you merely manage to *repress.*"

To a woman who rhapsodized about the
beauties of love the Master told the story of
Nasruddin, who was attempting to console his
dying wife in every possible way.

The woman opened her eyes and said, "It is
certain that this night will be my last. I shall not
see the sun again. Nasruddin, how will you take
my death?"

"How will I take your death? I will go mad."

Serious as her condition was, the woman could
not repress a smile. "Ah, you cunning fellow,"
she said. "I know you. You won't stay
unmarried for even a month after my death."

"What do you mean?" said Nasruddin
indignantly. "Of course I will go mad—but
I won't go that mad."

"Why do I do evil?"

"Because you are bewitched."

"By what?"

"The illusory thing you call your self."

"So how will evil cease?"

"Through understanding that the self as you know it does not exist—so it need not be protected."

"What is the cause of evil?"

"Ignorance," said the Master.

"And how is it dispelled?"

"Not by effort but by light. By understanding, not by action."

Later the Master added: "The sign of Enlightenment is Peace—you stop fleeing when you see you are only being pursued by the fantasies your fears have fabricated."

The Master had no illusions about what people
ordinarily call love. He recalled a conversation
he overheard in his younger days between a
politician and his friend:

"Did you know that our vice president is
planning to run against you in the coming
elections?"

"That scoundrel! I'm not one bit afraid.
Everyone knows that man isn't in jail only
because of his political connections."

"Our secretary is planning to announce his
candidacy too."

"What! Doesn't the man fear exposure for
embezzlement?"

"Well now! I was only joking. Actually I've just
met both of them and they're both supporting
your campaign."

"Now see what you've done! You've made me
say nasty things about two of the nicest men
in our association."

"Why do you never preach repentance?" said the preacher.

"It's the only thing I teach," said the Master.

"But I never hear you speak on sorrow for sin."

"Repentance isn't sorrow for the past. The past is dead and isn't worth a moment's grief. Repentance is a change of mind: a radically different vision of Reality."

The philosopher gave the Master a lengthy disquisition on "objective reality."

Said the Master, "What you know is not Reality but your perception of it. What you experience is not the world but your own state of mind."

"Can Reality ever be grasped then?"

"Yes—only by those who go beyond their thoughts."

"What sort of people are these?"

"Those who have lost the great projector, called the self; for when self is lost projection stops—and the world is seen in its naked loveliness."

When the Master heard someone say, "I'd like
my wife a lot better if she were a different kind
of woman," the Master recalled the time he was
admiring a sunset at sea.

"Isn't is lovely?" he exclaimed to the ship's bore
who was standing at the rail nearby.

"Yes," said the woman reluctantly. "But don't
you think there should be a little more pink on
the left?"

Said the Master, "Everyone looks lovely when
you shed your jaundiced expectations of what
they should look like."

"I pride myself on being a good judge of
character."

"Is that really something to be proud of?" said
the Master.

"Isn't it?"

"No. There's one defect a good judge has
in common with a bad judge: He judges."

"What depresses me is the utter ordinariness of
my existence. I haven't done a single important
thing in my life that the world would care to
notice."

"You are wrong to think that the attention of the
world is what gives importance to an action,"
said the Master.

A lengthy pause ensued.

"Well, I haven't done a single thing to influence
anyone for good or ill."

"You are wrong to think that influencing others
is what gives importance to an action," said the
Master.

"Well, then, what is it that gives importance
to an action?"

"Doing it for its own sake with the whole of
one's being. Then it becomes a non-profit,
God-like activity."

When one of his disciples was guilty of a serious lapse everyone expected the Master to give him some exemplary punishment.

When nothing was done for a whole month someone remonstrated with the Master: "We cannot ignore what has happened. After all, God has given us eyes."

"Yes," replied the Master, "and eyelids!"

"Why do you over-emphasize the value of
suffering in your sermons?" said the Master.

"Because it seasons us to face whatever life may
bring," was the preacher's reply.

The Master said nothing to that.

Later a disciple asked, "Exactly what does
suffering season us to face?"

"More suffering, presumably," said the Master
with a smile.

"Doesn't suffering season a person?"

"It's not the suffering that matters but a person's disposition, for suffering can sweeten or embitter just as the potter's fire can char the clay or season it."

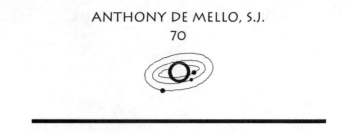

When asked why he never argued with anyone
the Master told of the old blacksmith who
confided to a friend that his blacksmith father
had wanted him to follow his profession
while his mother had set her heart on his
becoming a dentist. "And you know, I'm
glad my father had his way because if I had
become a dentist I would have starved to
death. And I can prove it."

"How?" asked the friend.

"Well, I've been in this smithy for thirty years
and not once in all that time has anyone asked
me to pull out a tooth."

"That," the Master concluded, "is the logic that
arguments are made of. When you see, you
need no logic."

"Why are you always at your prayers?" said the
Master.

"Because prayer takes a great load off my mind."

"Unfortunately, that is what it is wont to do."

"What's so unfortunate about it?"

"It distracts you from seeing who put the load
there in the first place," said the Master.

"You listen," said the Master, "not to discover, but to find something that confirms your own thoughts. You argue not to find the Truth but to vindicate your thinking."

And he told of a king who, passing through a small town, saw indications of amazing marksmanship everywhere. Trees and barns and fences had circles painted on them with a bullet hole in the exact center. He asked to see this unusual marksman. It turned out to be a ten-year-old child.

"This is incredible," said the king in wonder. "How in the world do you do it?"

"Easy as pie," was the answer. "I shoot first and draw the circles later."

"So you get your conclusions first and build your premises around them later," said the Master. "Isn't that the way you manage to hold on to your religion and to your ideology?"

It amused the Master to hear the exaggerated claims of modern science to change the Universe.

"In a conflict between human will and Nature, back Nature," he used to say.

"But can't we change anything in the Universe?"

"Not until we have learned to submit to it."

Every time the preacher mentioned God, the Master would say, "Keep God out of this."

The day came when the preacher could take it no longer. "I've always suspected you of being an atheist," he yelled. "WHY must I keep God out of this? . . . WHY?"

The Master gently told him the following story:

A priest went to console a widow at the death of her husband.

"Look what your God has done," screamed the woman.

"Death does not please God, my dear," replied the clergyman. "He deplores it just as much as you."

"Then why does he allow it?" she said angrily.

"There is no way we can know for God is Mystery."

"Then how come you know that death doesn't please him?" she yelled.

"Well, not really . . . we can assume . . ."

"SHUT UP!" screamed the widow. "Keep God out of this, will you!"

The activists were aggrieved that the Master thought they needed less action and more light.

"Light on what?" they wanted to know.

"On what life is all about," said the Master.

"We certainly know that life is to be lived for others," said the activists. "What more light do we need than that?"

"You need to understand what the preposition *for* means," said the Master.

The Master had a parable for the preacher:

> A centipede went to a wise old owl and
> complained of the gout. Each of its
> hundred legs ached. What could it do?
> After giving the matter serious thought
> the owl advised the centipede to
> become a squirrel. With only four legs
> it would have 96 percent of its pain
> removed.

> Said the centipede, "A splendid idea.
> Now tell me how I could go about
> becoming a squirrel."

"Don't bother me with that," said the
owl. "I only create policy around here."

"I long to find some solid ground, some firm
foundation for my life."

"Look at it like this," said the Master. "What
is the solid ground of the bird migrating across
continents? What is the firm foundation of the
fish carried by the river to the sea?"

An activist returned to find out what kind
of light he was still in need of.

"The light to know the difference between
a lover and an activist," the Master said.
"A lover participates in a symphony."

"And the activist?"

"Is caught up with the sound of his own drum,"
said the Master.

The Master never tired of reminding those who swore by their Scriptures that Truth cannot be grasped nor expressed by the conceptualizing mind.

He told of an executive who complained to his secretary about a phone call memorandum she had given him. "I can't read this," he said.

"I couldn't understand the caller on the phone very well," said the secretary. "So I didn't write it very clearly."

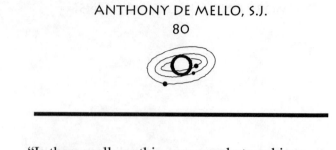

"Is there really nothing we can do to achieve Enlightenment?"

"Well," said the Master good-humoredly, "you could imitate the old woman who pressed against the wall of the carriage to speed the train along."

The preacher hotly contested the Master's teaching that there is nothing we can do to be Enlightened.

Said the Master, "But it is you, is it not, who preach that everything is a gift from God, that all our goodness is His grace?"

"Yes, but I also preach that God demands our cooperation."

"Ah! Like the man who chopped wood and demanded that his little son cooperate by doing the grunting," said the Master happily.

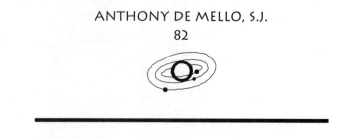

What newcomers found it hard to adjust to was
the humanity, the sheer ordinariness of the
Master. He enjoyed the good things of life and
the pleasures of the senses too much to fit into
their categories of what a holy man should be.

When one of them took this up with a disciple,
this is the reply he got:

"When God makes a Master, he does not
unmake the man."

A religious-minded disciple returned to the matter of Scripture. "Do you mean to say the Scriptures can give us no notion of God at all?"

"Any God that is contained in a notion is no God at all. That is why God is a Mystery—something you have no notion of," said the Master.

"Then what does Scripture offer us?"

In reply the Master told of the time he was dining in a Chinese restaurant when one of the musicians began to play a vaguely familiar melody whose name no one in the group could remember.

The Master summoned a smartly clad waiter and asked him to find out what the man was playing. He padded across the floor then returned to announce with pleasure, "Violin!"

"As your perception is, so will your action be.
The thing to change is not your action but your
outlook."

"What must I do to change it?"

"Merely understand that your present way
of looking is defective."

To illustrate his oft-repeated axiom, "You see
things as you are, not as they are," the Master
would tell of an eighty-one-year-old friend who
came to the monastery all wet and muddy.

"It's that creek a mile away from here," he said.
"I used to be able to jump right across in the
old days. But nowadays I always land in the
middle. I just hadn't noticed that the creek has
been getting wider."

To which the Master himself added, "Nowadays
I realize, each time I bend, that the ground is
further away than it used to be when I was
young."

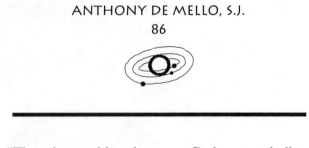

"There is one thing that even God cannot do,"
said the Master to a disciple who feared to give
offense.

"What?"

"He cannot please everyone," said the Master.

"What you need is awareness," said the Master to the religious-minded disciple, "awareness, awareness, awareness."

"I know; so I seek to be aware of God's presence."

"God-awareness is a fantasy, for you have no notion of what God is like. Self-awareness is what you need."

Later he said, "If God is Love, then the distance between God and you is the exact distance between you and the awareness of yourself."

When someone insisted that there could be only one *absolutely* right answer to any given moral question, the Master said:

"When people sleep in a damp place they get lumbago. But that's not true of fish.

"Living on a tree can be perilous and trying on the nerves. But that's not true of monkeys.

"So of these three, fish and monkeys and human beings, whose habitat is the right one—absolutely?

"Human beings eat flesh, buffaloes grass, and trees feed on the earth. Of these three, whose taste is the right one—absolutely?"

A young man eagerly described what he
dreamed of doing for the poor.

Said the Master, "When do you propose
to make your dream come true?"

"As soon as the opportunity arrives."

"Opportunity never arrives," said the Master.
"It's here."

An affluent man once told the Master that, try as he might, he simply couldn't stop the compulsion to make money.

"Even at the cost of enjoying life, alas," said the Master.

"I shall leave the enjoyment of life for my old age."

"If you ever live to have one," said the Master as he recounted the story of the highwayman who said, "Your money or your life!" Said the victim, "Take my life. I'm saving my money for my old age."

For another wealthy man who endangered his
health in his zeal for making money the Master
told the story of the miser who was being taken
to his grave.

Suddenly he came to consciousness, sized up
the situation, and made a quick decision: "I'd
better stay put—or else I'll have to pay the
funeral bill."

"Most people would rather save their money
than their lives," was the Master's conclusion.

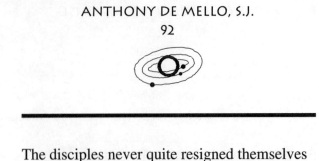

The disciples never quite resigned themselves to the Master's teaching that one had to "do" nothing to change or be Enlightened.

"What can you DO to dispel darkness?" he would say. "Darkness is the absence of light. Evil, the absence of awareness. What does one DO to an absence?"

"My parents told me to beware of you," said
a newcomer.

The Master smiled. "Beware, my dear, be very,
very careful, and you will meet the fate of your
cautious parents—nothing very good or bad
will ever happen to you."

"I don't know if I can trust this man," said
a newcomer.

Said an experienced disciple, "The Master
wouldn't have us trust a single word he says—
he urges us to doubt, to question, to challenge
everything."

Later he added, "It isn't the Master's words
I fear. It's his presence. His words bring light
but his presence burns you up."

When someone expressed her hatred for the oppressors of her country, the Master replied, "Never allow anyone to drag you down so low as to make you hate them."

"If you search for God you search for ideas—
and miss the Reality," said the Master.

He then told of the monk who complained
about the cell he had been given. "I wanted a
cell from where I could contemplate the stars.
In the one I have a stupid tree blocks out the
view."

Now it was while gazing at that particular tree
that Enlightenment had come to the previous
occupant of the cell.

"What does your Master teach?"

"Nothing."

"Then what on earth does he offer?"

"As much as you wish to take of his silence;
and his love; and of the rays of the myriad suns
that shine in the skies within him; and through
every leaf and blade of grass."

"Everyone knows I am fearless," said the governor, "but I confess to the fear of one thing: death. What is death?"

"How should I know?"

"But you are an Enlightened Master!"

"Maybe. But not a dead one yet."

A scientist showed the Master a documentary film on the achievements of modern science.

"Today we are able to irrigate a desert," he exulted, "harness the power of Niagara Falls, detect the composition of a distant star and the makeup of an atom. Our conquest of Nature will soon be complete."

The Master was impressed but pensive.

Later, this is what he said:

"Why conquer Nature? Nature is our friend. Why not spend all that energy in overcoming the one single enemy of the human race—fear?"

When some of his disciples spoke in praise of a well-known religious leader, the Master held his peace.

When asked about this later, he said, "The man wields power over others—he is no religious leader."

"What then is a religious leader's function?"

"To inspire, not to legislate," said the Master. "To awaken, not coerce."

It baffled the disciples to hear the Master
say that evil, when viewed from a higher
perspective, is good, that sin is a doorway
to grace.

So he told them the story of Carthage, a thorn
in the flesh of Ancient Rome. When Rome
finally razed Carthage to the ground she found
rest, grew flabby, and decayed.

"If all evil were to disappear," concluded the
Master, "the human spirit would rot."

"What sort of penance shall I do, given the
enormity of my crimes?"

"Understand the ignorance that caused them,"
said the Master.

Later he added, "It is thus you will understand
and forgive both others and yourself and
stop calling for the revenge you refer to as
punishment or penance."

The Master claimed that a major reason for
unhappiness in the world is the secret pleasure
people took in being miserable.

He told of a friend who said to his wife, "Why
don't you get away and have a good time,
darling?"

"Now, dear, you know perfectly well that I never
enjoy a good time!" was her irritated reply.

A business executive asked what the Master thought was the secret of successful living.

Said the Master, "Make one person happy each day."

As an afterthought he added, "Even if that person is yourself."

A minute passed and he said, "Especially if that person is yourself."

When the governor came on a visit, the Master took the occasion to protest against the censorship he had imposed on the press.

Said the governor sharply, "You have no idea how dangerous the press has become lately."

Said the Master, "Only the suppressed word is dangerous."

Once, in the course of a talk he gave, the Master
quoted from an ancient poet.

A young woman came up later to say she would
rather he had quoted from the Scriptures.

"Did that pagan author whom you quoted really
know God?" she said.

"Young woman," said the Master severely,
"if you think that God is the author of the book
you call the Scriptures, I would have you know
he is also the author of a much earlier work
called Creation."

Someone asked the Master why he seemed
so wary of religion. Wasn't religion the finest
thing humanity possessed?

The Master's reply was enigmatic: "The best
and the worst—that's what you get from
religion."

"Why the worst?"

"Because people mostly pick up enough religion
to hate but not enough to love."

"In spirituality it isn't effort that counts," said
the Master, "but surrender."

"When you fall into the water and don't know
how to swim you become frightened and say,
'I must not drown, I must not drown,' and begin
to thrash about with arms and legs—and,
in your anxiety, swallow more water and
eventually drown. Whereas if you would let go
of your thoughts and efforts and allow yourself
to go down to the bottom, your body would
come back to the surface on its own . . . That's
spirituality!"

"Sincerity is not enough," the Master would frequently say. "What you need is honesty."

"What's the difference?" someone asked.

"Honesty is a never-ending openness to the facts," said the Master. "Sincerity is believing one's own propaganda."

One day the Master said, "You are not ready to 'fight' evil until you are able to see the good it does."

This left the disciples in considerable confusion, which the Master made no attempt to clear.

The following day he offered them this prayer that was found scrawled on a piece of wrapping paper in the Ravensbruck concentration camp:

"Lord, remember not only the men and women of good will but all those of ill will. Do not only remember all the suffering they have subjected us to. Remember the fruits we brought forth thanks to this suffering—our comradeship, our loyalty, our humility, our courage and generosity, the greatness of heart that all of this inspired. And when they come to judgment, let all these fruits we have borne be their reward and their forgiveness."

A disciple put it to the Master point blank one
day: "Have you attained holiness?"

"How should I know?" was the reply.

"Who would know, if you didn't?"

Said the Master: "Ask a normal person if he
is normal, and he will assure you he is. Ask a
crazy person if he is normal—and he will assure
you he is!"

And with that, he gave a mischievous laugh.

Later he said: "If you realize you're crazy,
you're not so crazy after all, are you? If you
suspect you're holy, you're not so holy after all,
are you? Holiness is always unself-conscious."

A newcomer, dissatisfied, said to one of the disciples, "I really must know if the Master is holy or not."

"Why should it matter?" said the disciple.

"Why should I follow him if he himself has not arrived at holiness?"

"And why should you follow him if he has? According to the Master, the day you follow someone you cease to follow Truth."

Then he added, "Sinners often speak the truth. And saints have led people astray. Examine what is said, not the one who says it."

Asked about the Providence of God, the Master told the story of two Jews who had fallen upon hard times.

"I know that God will provide," said one with great conviction.

"I only wish He would provide UNTIL He provides," said the other.

One of the evil effects of religion, according to the Master, is that it has split humanity into sects.

He loved to tell of the little boy who asks his little girlfriend, "Are you a Presbyterian?"

"No," said the little one loftily, "we belong to another abomination!"

When asked why seeing was so difficult this
is what the Master said:

> When Sam returned from Europe, his
> partner in Men's Underwear Ltd. asked
> him eagerly: "Were you able to visit
> Rome, Sam?"
>
> "Yes, of course!"
>
> "And did you see the pope?"
>
> "See the pope? I had a private audience
> with him."
>
> "You don't say!" exclaimed his partner
> in wide-eyed wonder. "What's he like?"
>
> "Oh, I'd say he's a size thirteen and
> a half," said Sam.

When a group of pilgrims complained that the
Master had offended their religious sentiments,
he laughingly explained that what he had really
hurt was their ego.

And he told them of a bishop who declared
the Madonna of the Shrine to be the patroness
of the diocese; whereupon all the devotees
of the Madonna of the Temple who had
unsuccessfully lobbied to have that honor
conferred on their own candidate took out a
procession in protest and declared a one-day
fast in reparation to the Madonna of the
Temple.

"Was it the Madonna who was offended or their
so-called religious sentiments?" asked the
Master.

A philosopher who couldn't quite grasp what
the Master meant by Awareness asked him
to define it.

"It cannot be defined," said the Master.

"Is it thought?"

"Not concepts and reflections," said the Master,
"but the kind of thought you exercise in
moments of great danger when your brain stops
dead—or in moments of great inspiration."

"And what kind of thinking is that?"

"Thinking with your body-brain-being," said the
Master.

Said the Master:

"There are those who think that problems are solved through effort. These people merely succeed in keeping themselves and others busy.

"Problems are only solved through awareness. In fact, where there is awareness, problems do not arise."

The preacher was on a tour to various foreign countries.

Said the disciples, "Do you think travel will broaden his mind?"

"No," said the Master. "It will merely spread his narrow-mindedness over a wider area."

The Master laughed at people who set
themselves up as spiritual guides for others
when they themselves were lost and confused.

He loved to tell of the author who wrote
A Guide for Pedestrians and was run over
the day the book was released.

When a dictator came to power the Master was arrested in the act of distributing leaflets at the street corner in defiance of censorship regulations.

At headquarters his knapsack proved to contain nothing more harmful than blank sheets of paper.

"What does this mean?" the police demanded.

The Master smiled and replied, "The people know what it means."

This story became well known throughout the country, so the local priests weren't one bit amused when, years later, the Master was found distributing blank sheets of paper within the temple precincts.

The Master clearly advocated "thought-free,"
"knowledge-less" contemplation as a means
to know Reality.

"How can one *know* Reality without
knowledge?" a disciple asked.

"The way one knows music," said the Master.

A millionaire came to the monastery vowing
he would teach "the old fool something of the
pleasures of the world so that he doesn't waste
his life in the deprivations of a monastery."

The disciples, knowing as they did the Master's
delight in the good things of life, laughed aloud
when they heard this. "Teaching the old fool
how to enjoy life," said one of them, "would
be like giving a fish a bath."

"Is it possible to see the divine?"

"You are seeing it right now."

"Why do we not recognize it?"

"Because you distort it by means of thought."

When they failed to comprehend, he said:

"When the cold winds blow water turns into hardened blocks called ice.

"When thought intervenes Reality is fragmented into a million hardened pieces called 'things.' "

The Master was asked: "How does one find God in action?"

He replied, "By loving the action wholeheartedly, regardless of the fruit it brings."

When this proved somewhat difficult for the disciples he told them of a man who bought a painting for a million dollars, then framed the canceled check.

"What he really loved was not Art," said the Master, "but Status."

"Speak to us about sex."

"Sex," said the Master, "for those who know it, is divine."

"Those who know it?"

Said the Master:

"The frog sits next to the flowers quite unconscious of the honey found by the bee."

"What is the greatest obstacle to Truth?"

"A reluctance to face the facts," said the Master.

By way of illustration he told of the overweight
woman who stepped off the scales and said,
"According to this height-weight table here,
I should be about six inches taller."

Later he told of another woman who finally got
around to doing something about her weight:
she gave up stepping on the scales!

To all firm believers—whether their beliefs
were religious, political, or economic, it
mattered not—the Master had this one message:

"What you need is not security but the daring
of the gambler; not solid ground to stand on
but the dexterity of the swimmer."

One clear, starry night the Master gave his
disciples the benefit of his studies in astronomy:

"That is the Spiral Galaxy of Andromeda," he
said. "It is as large as our Milky Way. It sends
out rays of light that, at a speed of 186,000
miles a second, take two and a half million
years to get to us. It consists of a hundred
thousand million suns, many larger than our
own sun."

Then, after a moment's silence, he said with
a grin, "Now that we have put ourselves into
perspective, let's go to bed."

"I seek the peace that comes from death to the self."

Said the Master, "Who is it that seeks this peace?"

"I."

"Now how will your 'I' ever get a peace that will only come alive when your 'I' has died?"

Later he told them the following tale:

> When the old dealer in buttons and ribbons died, he left, to everyone's surprise, an enormous fortune in insurance policies.
>
> This, however, did not console his widow who wailed: "My poor, poor husband—all his life he labored day and night in dire poverty. And now that God has sent us this fortune, he's not there to enjoy it!"

The Master once quoted the celebrated words of the Bhagavad Gita in which the Lord urges the devotee to plunge into the thick of battle, while maintaining a peaceful heart at the lotus feet of the Lord.

A disciple asked, "How can I achieve that?"

Said the Master: "Decide to be satisfied with any results your efforts may bring."

To explain how what most people seek is not the joy of awareness and activity but the comfort of love and approval the Master told of the time his youngest daughter demanded that he read from a book of fairy tales before she went to sleep each night.

One day he hit upon the idea of tape recording the stories. The little girl learned to manage the recorder and all went well for some days till one evening she thrust the storybook on her father.

"Now, darling," said the Master, "you know how to turn on the recorder."

"Yes," was the reply, "but I can't sit on its lap."

When a visitor announced he was leaving
because he couldn't take another word the
Master said, an older disciple was sympathetic.
"I know how you must feel," he said. "For years
I avoided the man because his words were like
crates that shipped rampaging wild beasts
straight from the jungle into my tidy little
garden. I would much, much rather have gone
to preachers whose words shipped neat white
bones from one graveyard to another."

The Master chided a disciple who was forever landing himself in trouble because of his compulsion to tell the truth.

"But mustn't we always tell the truth?" the man protested.

"Ah no! The truth is sometimes best withheld."

When challenged to give an instance of this the Master told of a mother-in-law who had come for a week and stayed for a month.

The young couple finally hit upon a plan to rid themselves of the woman. "I'll serve soup tonight," said the wife to her husband, "and we'll start arguing. You claim it has too much salt, and I'll say it doesn't have enough. If mother agrees with you I'll get mad and order her out and if she agrees with me you get furious and order her to leave."

Soup was served. The fight became vicious when the wife said, "Mother, how about it; is the soup too salty or not?"

The crusty old lady dipped her spoon into the soup, lifted it to her lips, tasted it carefully, paused for a moment's thought, and said, "Suits me."

When a disciple declared his intention of becoming a preacher, the Master wouldn't hear of it. All he said was, "Wait, you are not ready."

A year went by, then two, then five, then ten, and still the Master held on to his prohibition.

One day the disciple said, "Couldn't I do some little good even though I am not ready?"

Said the Master, "How effective will a hunter be who shoots before he has a bullet in his gun?"

To explain why holiness is unself-conscious
the Master told of an alcoholic friend who had
sworn he would never drink again. One day,
suffering from the pangs of thirst, he asked the
bartender for a lemonade. And, while it was
being prepared, he whispered, "And could you
put a little whisky into it while I'm not
looking?"

The social activist was all eagerness to change the structures of society.

"Fine," said the Master. "But what we need is not just ACTION that will bring about change but SIGHT that will bring about love."

"So according to you changing structures is a waste of time."

"No, no. Changed structures can protect love— they cannot generate it," said the Master.

"The trouble with you," said the Master to the preacher, "is that everything you say is absolutely true—and hollow. Your people seek Reality. All you offer them is words."

When the preacher demanded to know what he meant, the Master said, "You are like the man who received a letter from an installment company that said: 'Will you kindly send us the full amount you owe us?'

"His reply was prompt and clear: 'The full amount I owe you is one thousand five hundred dollars.' "

The Master sent a strongly worded protest to the governor about his brutal handling of an antiracism demonstration.

The governor wrote to say that he had only done his duty.

Said the Master: "Each time a stupid man does something he should be ashamed of, he declares it to be his duty."

The Master once told of two society matrons,
one of whom said to the other, "I met your
husband the other day. Heavens, what a brilliant
man! I suppose he knows everything."

"Don't be silly," said the other. "He doesn't
suspect a thing!"

Said the Master, "That's what the scholar is
likely to be: someone who knows everything
there is to know about Reality and doesn't even
suspect its existence."

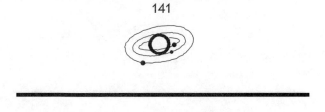

"Why do you travel so little?" a reporter asked.

"To look into the face of just one person or thing every day of the year and never fail to find something new in it—that is a greater adventure by far than any that travel can offer," said the Master.

When the Master heard a disciple speak
disparagingly of the greed and violence of
"people out there in the world," he said,
"You remind me of the wolf who was going
through a virtuous phase; when he saw a cat
chasing a mouse he turned to a fellow wolf
and said indignantly: 'Isn't it time someone
did something to stop this hooliganism?' "

"What is the biggest obstacle to Enlightenment?"

"Ignorance."

"Is there just one type of ignorance or are there many?"

"Many," said the Master. "For instance your particular brand of ignorance demands that you search for Enlightenment."

The Master once told of a woman who asked
her dentist for the third time to grind down her
denture because "it does not fit."

"If I do as you say I fear the teeth won't fit your
mouth," said the dentist.

"Who said anything about my mouth?"
exclaimed the irritated woman. "The teeth don't
fit in the glass."

And the Master concluded, "Your beliefs may
suit your mind, but do they fit the facts?"

In his younger days the Master had left his
home in quest of wisdom.

His parting words were, "The day I find it
I shall let you know."

Many years later letting them know seemed
quite unimportant. That's when he knew that,
all unknown to himself, he had indeed found it.

Speaking of religious leaders who sought to impress others by their outward behavior and dress, the Master told his disciples this one:

As a drunkard staggered home he thought of an ingenious way to conceal his condition from his wife: He would sit in his study and read a book; who ever heard of a drunken person reading a book?

When his wife demanded to know what he was doing there in the corner of his study, he replied cheerfully, "Reading, my dear."

"You're drunk!" said his wife. "Shut that suitcase and come down to dinner."

When the Master remarked on the irrationality
of a visitor's beliefs, he replied grandly,
"I believe because it is irrational."

"Shouldn't you rather say: I believe because
I am irrational?" said the Master.

"How does one attain to happiness?"

"By learning to be content with whatever one gets."

"Then can't one ever desire anything?"

"Yes, one can," said the Master, "provided one has the attitude of an anxious father I once met in a delivery ward. When the nurse said, 'I know you were hoping to get a boy, but it's a baby girl,' the man replied, 'Oh, it doesn't matter really, because I was hoping that it would be a girl if it wasn't a boy.' "

The Master once overheard a disciple say to a visitor, "I have been honored for, while hundreds were sent away, the Master singled me out for acceptance as a disciple."

Later the Master said to him privately, "Let's get one thing clear from the start: If you were chosen rather than the others, it is only because your need is greater than theirs."

On the subject of the moral upbringing of
children, the Master once had this to say:

"When I was a teenager, my father warned
me about certain places in the city.

> He said, 'Don't ever go into a night
> club, son.'

> 'Why not, father?' said I.

> 'Because you'll see things that you
> shouldn't.'

"This, of course, aroused my curiosity. And
at the first opportunity I got I went into a night
club."

The disciples asked, "And did you see
something you shouldn't have?"

"I certainly did," said the Master. "I saw my
father."

"My former Master taught me to accept birth and death."

"Then what have you come to me for?" asked the Master.

"To learn to accept what lies in between."

A disciple was convinced she was selfish, worldly, unspiritual. However, after a week's stay in the monastery, the Master pronounced her spiritually fit and healthy.

"But isn't there *something* I can do to be as spiritual as the other disciples?"

To that the Master replied:

> Listen to this: A man bought a car once and, after careful computation over six months, came to the conclusion that he was not getting the phenomenally high mileage so often attributed to such cars. He took it to a mechanic who checked the car and declared it to be in perfect condition.
>
> "But isn't there *something* I can do to increase its mileage?" said the man.
>
> "Well, yes," said the mechanic. "You can do what most car owners do."
>
> "What's that?"
>
> "Lie about it."

When asked what he did for his disciples, the Master said, "What a sculptor does for the statue of a tiger: He takes a block of marble and pounds away at anything that doesn't look like a tiger."

When his disciples later asked what exactly he meant, the Master said, "My task is to hammer away at everything that isn't you: every thought, feeling, attitude, compulsion that adheres to you from your culture and your past."

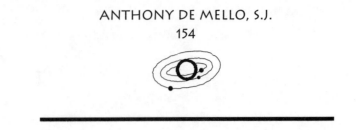

One of the Master's reservations about religious leaders was this: they fostered blind credulity in the faithful to the point that, even when some of them dared to raise a question, it was always within the narrow limits of their belief.

There was once a preacher, he said, who honestly sought to get his people to question what he said. So he resorted to this device: He told them the story of a decapitated martyr who walked with his head in his hands till he came to a wide river. Then, since he needed both hands for swimming, he put his head into his mouth and swam safely across.

There was a moment of unquestioning silence, then, to the preacher's delight, one man stood up to question that: "He couldn't have done that!"

"Why not?" asked the preacher hopefully.

"Because," said the man, "if he had his head in his mouth he wouldn't have been able to breathe."

"Happiness is a butterfly," said the Master.
"Chase it and it eludes you. Sit down quietly and
it alights upon your shoulder."

"So what do I do to get happiness?"

"Stop pursuing it."

"But is there nothing I can do?"

"You might try sitting down quietly—if you
dare!"

Like Jesus centuries before him, the Master
warned people about religion because, left to
itself, it sanctified the blind observance of the
law. This is how he put it:

A commanding officer was asking some
recruits why walnut was used for the butt of
a rifle.

"Because it has more resistance," said one man.

"Wrong!"

"Because it has more elasticity," said another.

"Wrong again!"

"Perhaps because it has a better shine than other
woods," said a third.

"Don't be a fool," said the C.O. "Walnut is used
because it is laid down in the regulations."

"Do you believe in the existence of God?" asked
the fanatical believer.

Said the Master, "I shall answer your question
if you answer mine: Is your chair the first one
to the left?"

"To the left of what?"

"The existence of what?" said the Master.

To show his disciples the absurdity of religious authority that came from any source other than personal worth and competence, the Master told of the worker who went to a matrimonial agency.

"Is this a union shop?" he asked.

"Yes, certainly."

He picked out the picture of a beautiful twenty-five-year-old and said, "I'll take her."

"No, you have to take this lady," said the agency director, showing him the picture of a greying woman of fifty.

"Why do I have to take her?"

"Because she," said the director, "has seniority."

"How long does the present last—a minute,
a second?"

"Much less and much more," said the Master.
"Less, because the moment you focus on it,
it's gone.

"More, because if you ever get into it, you will
stumble upon the Timeless, and will know what
Eternity is."

Said the Master:

"When you were in the womb you were silent.
Then you were born and began to talk, talk,
talk—till the day you are laid in your tomb.
Then you will once again be silent.

"Capture the silence that was there in the womb
and will be there in the tomb and even now
underlies this interval of noise called life; that
silence is your deepest essence."

"What's so original about this man?" asked a
visitor. "All he gives you is a hash of stories,
proverbs, and sayings from other Masters."

A woman disciple smiled. She once had a cook,
she said, who made the most wonderful hash in
the world.

"How on earth do you make it, my dear? You
must give me the recipe."

The cook's face glowed with pride. She said,
"Well, ma'am, I'll tell yer: beef's nothin';
pepper's nothin'; onion's nothin': but when
I throws *myself* into the hash—that's what
makes it what it is."